HERBERT MURRILL

CARILLON

MUSIC DEPARTMENT

OXFORD
UNIVERSITY PRESS

To Arnold Richardson

CARILLON

HERBERT MURRILL

Printed in Great Britain

OXFORD UNIVERSITY PRESS, MUSIC DEPARTMENT, GREAT CLARENDON STREET, OXFORD OX2 6DP

cresc.

[Gt.]

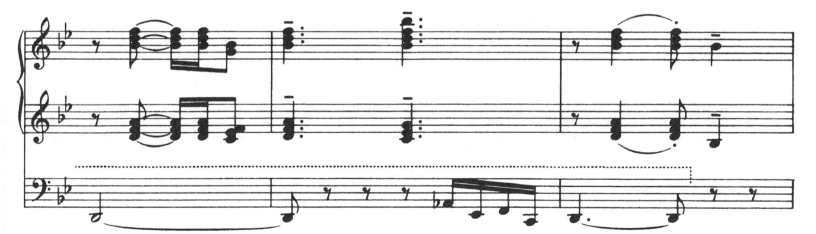

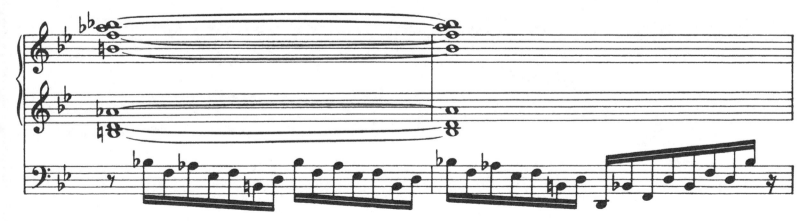

* On some instruments it may be found desirable to play this and the similar passage on page 7 an octave higher than written.

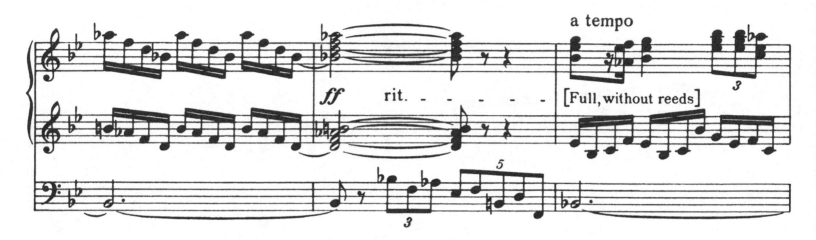

Allargando
[Full without Reeds: Sw. closed]

[Reeds]

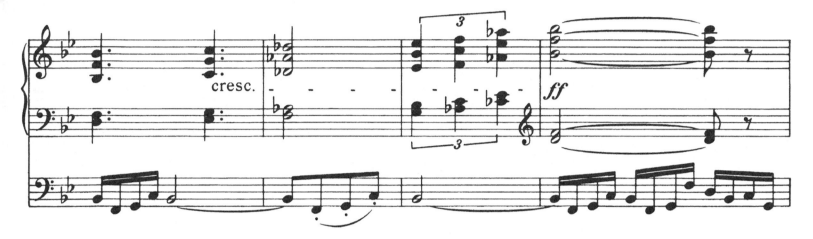

cresc. _ _ _ _ _ _ _ _ *ff*

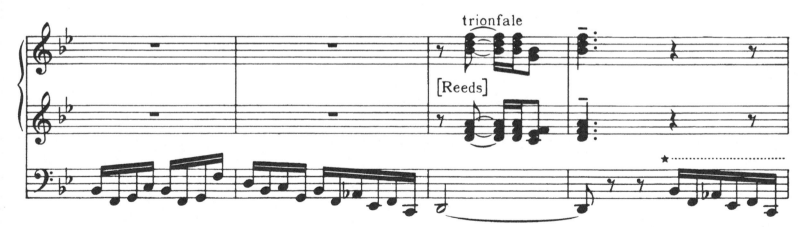

trionfale

[Reeds]

Più allarg al _ _ Lento

fff

[Close Swell, and open on final
chord. If crescendo pedal is
available, play *pp* ◁ *fff*]